'Those who contemplate
the beauty of the earth
find reserves of strength
that will endure
as long as life lasts.'

Rachel Carson, *Silent Spring*

Creative team

Editor-in-chief
Carole Bamford

Creative Director
Claudie Dubost

Editorial Director
Imogen Fortes

Contributing Editor
Sophie Richardson

Production Coordinator
Matt Gorman

Contributors

Words
Carole Bamford
Leonora Bamford
Imogen Fortes
Katriona Jones
Satish Kumar
Sophie Richardson
Jez Taylor
Michael Townsend Williams
Francesca White

Recipes
Adam Caisley
Gaven Fuller
Katriona Jones
Lydia Lishman

Images

Photography
Lucasz Augusciak
Shine Bhola
Benjamin J Borley
Helen Cathcart
Jim Marsden
Lizzie Mayson
Martin Morrell

Styling
Linda Berlin
Claudie Dubost
Frankie Unsworth

Illustrations
Hugo Guinness
Blandine Pannequin

Printed in the United Kingdom at
Wood Mitchell Printers on 100% recycled paper

Colour reproduction by BORN London

Cover photography by Martin Morrell

@seed_magazine

Contents

Seed likes

A BOOK

'No One is Too Small to Make a Difference'
by Greta Thunberg

|

A PLACE

Rineia
Greece

|

A POEM

'Aedh Wishes for the Cloths of Heaven'
by W. B. Yeats

|

A TABLE

Conca del Sogno,
Amalfi Coast, Italy

|

AN EXHIBITION

Mary Quant
at The Victoria and Albert Museum, London

Editor's letter

PORTRAIT Martin Morrell

Over the past year, we have all watched and listened as the conversations around the future of our planet have grown louder, more passionate, more fervent. The tone of the language has evolved: we can no longer refer to a climate change; we are in the midst of a climate emergency and we urgently need to halt the crisis that is gathering force at an alarming rate. But what strikes me most about the events of the last year is that it has taken the words of a 16-year-old to invite the world to sit up and listen. Greta Thunberg has divided opinion, but on whichever side one falls, the lesson to be drawn from her impassioned voice is that we must listen to our children. It is their future that is in our hands and we need to protect it and safeguard the planet they will one day inherit.

So why add another voice to the conversation? Why launch *Seed*, a magazine devoted to living more sustainably? And for me the answer is simple: it is by arming ourselves with knowledge and an awareness of the reasons to make a change that we can incite action.

By sharing the voices of others who live and work in a conscious way – artisans, artists, makers and thinkers; pioneers in the fields of sustainability, farming, craft, design, wellness and travel – we hope to inspire you to make small changes to your own choices. It is through collective responsibility that we can drive change on a wider scale and impact the future of our planet, like sowing a seed that will one day grow and flourish into a plant.

Seed is above all a celebration – of the beauty in nature and of all that it provides for us. I hope that it might remind you of why we need to look after what we have: to nourish and care for our soil, our land and our planet. And I hope that you are inspired to plant seeds of your own.

– Carole Bamford

CAROLE BAMFORD INTERVIEWS

PATRICK HOLDEN

PHOTOGRAPHY Portrait by Benjamin J Borley for TEDxExeter;
Landscape by Martin Morrell

Patrick Holden is the founder of the Sustainable Food Trust, a charitable organisation that strives for a better food and farming system, for people and planet. He was the founding chairman of British Organic Farmers in 1982, before joining the Soil Association, where he worked for nearly 20 years and during which time the organisation led the development of organic standards. He is Patron of the UK Biodynamic Association and was awarded the CBE for services to organic farming in 2005.

1- You founded the Sustainable Food Trust to drive change and move towards a more sustainable food production and farming system around the world. What do you mean by the term 'sustainable'?

There was a definition included in the UN's Brundtland report, published by the World Commission on Environment and Development in 1987, which stated that 'sustainable development is development that meets the needs of the present without compromising the ability of future generations to meet their own needs'. Although that remains a reasonable definition,

it's not precise enough for food and agriculture. I believe it's very important to use language exactly and to define your terms, and I think that what's happened to the word 'sustainable' is that it's been hijacked by lots of different organisations, who've all used it loosely, without properly defining it. That is why we've put so much work over the years into developing a more precise definition.

Nearly 40 years ago I was involved in setting out what a group of us believed was a means of defining sustainability, which was to draw up the organic standards. In a way what we did was to state that anything less than the farming

'To maintain our soil fertility and secure a healthy sustainable food production system for future generations, we need to farm in rotation.'

practices set out by the standards laid down, wasn't sustainable. Does that standard work today as an adequate definition of sustainability? In some ways it does but in other ways it's too binary. The best way, the *new* way to define sustainability needs to be through measurement. We need to create a sort of 'stairway to heaven' whereby every step on the ladder towards sustainable farming practice is acknowledged and possibly scored.

2- So many of the wider conversations around sustainability and the future of food production now focus on the farming of livestock and the questions around meat consumption, but for me what's not being discussed enough is the health of our soil. Sustainable food production and feeding future generations will not be possible if we don't look after our soil. Do you feel the public education and messages coming out of these conversations need to change?

I agree you're right to put so much emphasis on soil. As Sir Albert Howard said in his prophetic book *An Agriculture Testament*, which was first published in 1940, 'the health of the soil, plants, animals and people is one and indivisible'. His inspiration was the peasant farmers in northwest India who were composting and farming like you farm at Daylesford, and he observed that when you look after the soil and make it fertile and healthy, that is reflected in the health of the plants and animals that depend on that soil, as well as in human health. This was based on his observations of the Hunza people who lived to 100 and were feared fighters. He made the connection between their health and the quality of their soil and predicted that if a nation industrialised

its agriculture, it would compromise the mental and physical health of its people. That's exactly what's come to pass.

After the Second World War nitrogen fertilisers became widely available and farmers realised that if they put these on the fields, they could avoid having to rotate their crops. What they hadn't realised, however, was that these traditional methods of rotation were not just providing nitrogen, they were providing carbon, which is vital for soil quality and fertility. Our UK soils were once carbon rich but we've been mining the accumulated fertility of generations. Now we need to put it back.

Nutrient density is a key emergent issue in our food system. We're all encouraged to eat our five-a-day, but if we're eating fruit and veg whose nutrition is perhaps 50 per cent of what it used to be, then actually we're missing the point. Most of the vegetables many of us eat today are from supermarkets, grown in chemical monocultures. Livestock and crop rotation are essential in producing healthy fruit and vegetables and there are light years of difference between the nutrient quality of organic vegetables grown at farms where their soil health is monitored, fed and nurtured, and the industrially-produced vegetables you buy at supermarkets.

3- How was your own passion for sustainable farming and latterly for campaigning about it ignited?

On the former, it was feeling connected to nature. Even though I grew up in London, we took childhood holidays in the Highlands and islands of Scotland and other places where I had a taste of nature from an early age. And for some reason, I developed an obsession with keeping animals so I had lots of pets – budgerigars, a mynah bird, hamsters, mice – I dug ponds and had newts in them. I was inspired by nature is the simple answer.

And on the second part; I come from a family of missionaries, so maybe it's epigenetic? I feel it's like a calling – if you see something and you're passionate about it, you have a certain responsibility to serve it. I do feel advocacy for a cause is a kind of service.

4- Plant-based diets, vegetarianism and veganism have seen a rapid and in some ways quite startling rise in popularity. Is plant-based eating the way we should be heading and is there a role for livestock farming within a sustainable food system?

Firstly, I think what needs to be said is that one can understand the psychology behind the drift towards vegan and vegetarian diets. If you look at industrial livestock production and are horrified by it – as you should be – then one can understand the shift. And if you then start to question whether there is any meat that you can buy confidently – aside from the likes of Daylesford, which is, in reality, physically and financially outside of the reach of many young people, then again, the argument is logical.

But these trends are largely based on an understandable revulsion at intensive livestock production, and what many people don't realise is that the vegan/vegetarian movements are going to create a major hurdle to the transition to sustainable farming systems. That's because livestock play an essential part in the building of soil carbon and soil fertility and to

producing nutrient-rich vegetables. To maintain our soil fertility and secure a healthy sustainable food production system for future generations, we need to farm in rotation, which includes a grass phase grazed by livestock to rebuild the fertility. This is the best way to grow crops full of nutrients.

To know which meats we can eat sustainably, we need to differentiate between the livestock that are part of the problem and those that are part of the solution. In the UK, grass-fed cows and sheep will play an essential role in future sustainable farming systems and we've got to get that message across.

5- And what would you say to people who are choosing to be vegetarian or vegan on environmental grounds?

I would tell them that they have undoubtedly heard that ruminant animals produce methane, which they do, and that methane is a potent greenhouse gas, which it is, however the carbon sequestration in grassland soils offsets these methane emissions. Also the methane cycle is as old as ruminant animals. It's a contained cycle – it's not adding new methane and that cycle is responsible for building some of the most fertile soils on the planet, such as the Corn Belt on the Great Plains in the US.

The real culprit in terms of global warming is fossil fuels. Nitrogen fertiliser is a big user of fossil fuels, so I would say identify the farming systems that don't use nitrogen fertiliser, are based on pasture- and grass-fed animals and crop rotations, such as organic, and are in fact making a positive impact on our planet.

6- We are in the midst of a crippling health crisis in this country and our food isn't giving us the nutrition we need. Our food industry can send very confusing messages to consumers and often the cheapest food is the least healthy, or is in fact damaging our bodies. Meanwhile our Mediterranean neighbours have some of the healthiest diets in the world. Where do you think we are going wrong, why have we lost the nutrition you're referring to, and is there a solution in your opinion?

To a degree it's cultural. Italy, France and Germany, for example, are connected to the land: they have smaller farms than we do and there's a strong tradition of food in these countries. The UK and the US led the industrialisation of agriculture; they urbanised and lost that connection with their food production. Farmers in this country have become commodity slaves – at the mercy of market demands – and there's a parallel slavery in the food industry: profit; keeping shareholders happy; and customers wanting cheap food. It's a tyranny and everybody is losing.

In my opinion we need to place greater value on food. Unless we transform our food and farming systems within the next 10–15 years we're going to face irreversible climate change and a public health catastrophe which is already starting to show in infertility, in cancers and in the biodiversity crisis, which is only going to get worse. Unless we change our food systems, we won't have a planet fit to live on. I think we're near a tipping point. I've been involved with advocacy for more sustainable food systems since the 1970s and it's only now I feel that change is happening. Among young people, there's a shift in consciousness and we have a

'I feel that change is happening.
We have a generation who want to
do something different.'

generation who feel they want to do something different. I think that's really positive. But I think the action needs to be grounded in a better understanding of what the issues are and the reasons for taking it.

7- One of the biggest criticisms levied against organic food is that it's expensive and beyond the means of most people living in this country. How can we address this?

In almost every other aspect of life, we understand that if you want something of quality you have to pay the right price for it, except with food. We have a cultural disposition in this country to think that cheap food is a good thing and governments haven't stepped in – they too have been seduced by the concept of cheap food.

But if your farming system is industrial and degrades the biodiversity, the soil and causes air pollution you're simply using up nature's balance sheet: food looks cheap but actually it isn't. The Sustainable Food Trust produced a report called 'The Hidden Cost of UK Food', which identifies these costs and reveals the dishonesty of present food system pricing.

Much of the work I do is in trying to persuade DEFRA to correct these imbalances and dishonesties by introducing policy instruments – incentives and disincentives to ensure that the polluter pays and farmers who deliver benefits to public health – to the

soil and to biodiversity – are rewarded. If food were more honestly priced, the price of intensively-produced food would go up and sustainable organic food would come down. The point I am trying to make to the government is that we're already paying for this damage through higher National Health Service bills (through the Treasury), air pollution, or in water company bills (they clean up the nitrates in our water and pass on that cost to the consumer via higher water bills). We don't necessarily feel those costs in our pockets but we need to make them visible.

And then there are some costs that we're deferring until later, like climate change. Fossil fuel burning is the biggest contributor to climate change but a lot of that fossil fuel goes into agriculture, so agriculture and food are both colossal contributors to climate change. The carbon bank that we've released is vast but that's the one area where we could reverse climate change – by taking carbon dioxide out of the atmosphere, by recarbonising the soil – that's what goes on at Daylesford.

How do we communicate the organic message and circumnavigate some of the prejudice that has, in my opinion, been unfairly attached to this 'elitism'. You can understand why the elitism charge arose, but if you understand true cost accounting you can start to understand the real cost of food, rather than the cheap price, which is actually illusionary.

8- And what about farmers? Is a switch to organic farming economically viable for them?

For mainstream farmers, it's very difficult. If we want organic farming to go mainstream – and it must – we need a combination of the leadership shown by farms such as Daylesford, and government intervention in the form of redirected subsidies. And we need it fast.

TRUE BLUES

WORDS Sophie Richardson
PHOTOGRAPHY Lucasz Augusciak, Shine Bhola, Martin Morrell

INDIGOFERA
TINCTORIA

Indigofera tinctoria is the plant from which natural indigo pigment is derived, and one of the oldest sources of the dye in the world.

The legume thrives in tropical climates. Cultivation in India is mainly confined to the states of Tamil Nadu, Andhra Pradesh and Uttarakhand, although crops have previously flourished in the regions of Assam, Bihar, Uttar Pradesh, Gujarat and Madhya Pradesh.

The production of indigo dye is a closed cycle. Branches of the *Indigofera tinctoria* are harvested every four months. To extract the pigment the leaves are broken down through fermentation and the resulting liquid is then reduced and dried to create cakes of rich indigo dye. Once spent, the plants are returned to the land as a natural fertiliser; the ash from wood used to heat the vats is used in the preparation of the indigo cakes and the water used to extract the pigment is so clean it can go straight back onto crops.

Medicinally, the *Indigofera tinctoria* plant also has analgesic and anti-inflammatory properties and can be used to treat a wide range of disorders, including insect bites and stings, swelling, joint pain, arthritis and toothache.

Derived from the Greek word *indikon* meaning 'from India', indigo is the oldest natural dye in India and a colour that is woven into the fabric of the country's cultural and political history.

There are over 800 species of indigo plant in the world, but in India it is the leaves of the tropical *Indigofera tinctoria* that yield the rich blue pigment which has been used to dye textiles for over 4,000 years.

A sustainable crop, indigo was once grown widely across India, its cultivation enriching the soil of the fields in which it was rotated, and generating local employment in farming and traditional skills. However, the introduction of synthetic dyes in the late nineteenth century, coupled with a revolt across India against the forced cultivation of the crop, brought around a decline in commercial demand for true indigo, and today indigo dye in India is almost exclusively synthetic.

The impact can be felt across many areas. Within the rural artisan clusters that are dependent on textile dyeing, chemical discharge from the synthetic dyes pollutes not only the surrounding soil that is used to grow the village's crops, but also their sacred – and often scarce – water supply, which sustains the village. And from a cultural perspective, one of India's most cherished natural crafts is dying out, supplanted by a toxic chemical alternative.

It was these concerns – combined with a longstanding passion for India and natural dyes – that led to the launch of Nila House: a cultural centre of excellence, spearheaded by the Lady Bamford Foundation. At its heart is a desire to celebrate the wealth and diversity of traditional handicraft skills found across India; to inspire designers to use natural dyes in both traditional and innovative ways; and to support these crafts and their makers by offering a platform for artistic exchange, innovation and education.

Based in a beautiful heritage building constructed in the 1930s, Nila House encompasses a series of open studios, retail showrooms, an archive and research library, art gallery, textiles vault and artists-in-residence wing. And with its rich history of textiles, there is no better home for Nila House than the city of Jaipur.

Known as the 'Pink City' on account of its pink-hued architecture, the capital of Rajasthan has been a mecca for designers and jewellers for hundreds of years. Today this bustling city is home to thousands of traditional craftspeople as well as a dynamic generation of young creatives, who are inspired by the city's rich heritage and empowered by modern technology and international exchange.

Architecturally, Jaipur is the Maharani of Indian cities. Built in the early eighteenth century following the principles of Vastu Shastra, the city's neat symmetry and

ordered urban planning are in stark contrast to the thousands of stalls, shops and markets that sprawl across Jaipur's streets, with vegetable wallahs, gem traders, textile vendors and rickshaw drivers all jostling for space and attention.

Amidst the buzz of human activity are the many animals that roam the city's streets: troops of monkeys jump from the roofs above, elephants lumber slowly in the heat, stray dogs seek solace in the shade, while sacred cows weave precariously through the heaving traffic, unperturbed by the noise and chaos that surrounds them.

It is against this vibrant backdrop that Nila House stands; a handsome bungalow modestly constructed around a central courtyard. Once home to a wealthy Jaipur family, the property remained derelict for many years, becoming engulfed by nature and home only to monkeys and strays. Despite its state of ruin, the building stood nobly among the weeds, its restrained simplicity suggesting a perfect home for the cultural centre.

The renovation of the house was carried out by the architectural practice Studio Mumbai whose founder, Bijoy Jain, is known for his buildings that combine Indian tradition with modernity and reflect a deep concern for craft, sustainability and community.

Work on the house began in January 2018 and over the next few months the building was stripped back to its bones and then slowly restored, using locally-sourced natural materials and employing centuries'-old techniques.

The walls and ceilings have been plastered with natural lime, an ancient technique that allows the building to breathe, yet only a handful of houses are now constructed this way, with modern builders favouring the ease, speed and low cost of concrete. Lime paint was then applied to the walls, with a small amount of indigo added as a natural repellent against termites and mosquitos. Floors were laid with slabs of locally-sourced marble and limestone, and intricate stonework was chiselled by hand using ancient techniques.

The central section of the portico has been opened up to encourage air to circulate through the house, and Crittall doors have been added to the façade, allowing natural light to flood the rooms within. The interior has been left restrained and uncluttered, with simple furniture crafted from natural materials such as marble, bamboo, wood and jute.

The skills and traditions employed in the architectural restoration of Nila House mirror those that will be revived within the studios themselves. Craft-focused workshops and seminars will take place throughout the year, led by masters in their fields, including block printing and shibori dyeing, hand weaving and spinning, embroidery and ceramics.

The activities won't be confined to Nila House. Just an hour outside Jaipur, within the dyeing cluster of Bagru, lies Nila Dye Works, where there are vats of fermenting indigo for artisans to experiment and work with. The space is also open for visitors to come and experience first-hand the beauty and alchemy of indigo dyeing.

The process requires meditative precision and is only possible by hand. Lengths of yarns or fabric are lowered into a deep vat containing fermented indigo pigment mixed with pH-neutral water and natural bacteria. Once stirred and dipped, there follows a magical moment when the cloth or yarn is pulled out into the air, emerging as a yellowish-green colour, then, as the pigment oxidises, gradually turning to blue.

Different shades and depths of blue are achieved according to the number of times a fabric is dipped in the dye, from the palest clear blue (one or two dips), to a deep blue–black (a laborious ten dips). No matter how skilled the dyer, natural indigo is never uniform in colour and this liveliness is reinforced in the way it fades with wear and washing, its beauty increasing with age.

For those unable to visit the vats, the textiles archive at Nila House sells metres of indigo-dyed yarn and fabrics, alongside an archive of natural khadi cloth. Hand woven in villages across the country, khadi is steeped in Indian history and significance, and the simple white cloth, with all its irregularities and imperfections, is the embodiment of everything that Nila House aspires to revive and protect.

Elsewhere at Nila House there is a library containing research and writings on natural dyes, craft and design, and a basement gallery honouring India's rich legacy of textiles, as well as displaying specially-commissioned contemporary art works experimenting with indigo and natural dyes.

At the back of the building lies the residency wing and this will become home to a visiting roster of artists, makers and designers who have travelled to Jaipur to immerse themselves in the local culture and history, to learn from the craftspeople and to pass back their own experience and knowledge to the artisans. At the end of each residency, there will be an exhibition of the artists' works in their chosen discipline, be it textiles, sculpture, ceramics or paper.

Artistic exchange is at the heart of the foundation and each year Nila will embark on creative collaborations with designers for clothing and homeware collections, all exploring contemporary interpretations of traditional Indian craft. The first collaboration is with the British designer Anna Valentine, who has created a capsule collection of women's clothing that explores the many different hues of true indigo. Her collection of 20 pieces is undeniably European and contemporary in its shapes, and yet the techniques used are dense with Indian tradition – from layered silk kantha stitch jackets, handloom linen trousers and shibori-dyed khadi dresses, to racerback vests handmade in delicate silk, dyed in the palest shade of indigo, with intricate jaali stitch detail.

Each piece exemplifies the principles of slow fashion – timeless designs made to last for years, crafted from handwoven

and handmade textiles and celebrating skills that have been passed down through many generations. The desire to protect these valuable skills and traditions, while making them relevant and exciting for the next generation of makers, permeates everything that Nila House does.

This capsule collection will be available to buy at Nila House, alongside items for the home, including indigo dhurries woven in villages outside Jaipur, block-printed khadi nightwear, handwoven throws, and cushions festooned with tassels and pompoms made by women from rural communities in Rajasthan. The market presence curated by Nila House will directly support the artisans, feeding both money and market linkage directly back to the makers. For it is the artisans that Nila House ultimately seeks to support, and it is only by working from the grass roots up that the impact will be felt across all stages of the value chain. By working in partnerships with likeminded NGOs, the Lady Bamford Foundation is able to reach out to remote parts of India and engage with those who need the social and economic support most of all. Once the artisans' skills have been honed the works can be brought back to Nila House and promoted alongside others from across the country, representing the pinnacle of Indian craft techniques alive today.

The word 'nila' stems from a number of cultures in India and has different meanings: in Sanskrit it means 'blue', and 'temple'; in Pali, 'nest'; and in Tamil it means 'moon'. One word, many meanings, all capturing the spirit of Nila House: a place to gather, to share, to nurture and to celebrate the beauty and skills of India's traditional handicrafts, and the hands that create them.

Nila House opens on 17 October 2019.
For more information visit www.nilajaipur.com

How we choose to nourish ourselves, an act that should be so simple and natural, has become a subject laden with questions. A few generations ago, our food choices were guided by our senses – our tastes, our sense of smell – or simply what we could afford. Today, the way we eat has become a complex and often confusing issue.

At Seed we believe that eating well is about flavour, nutrition and nourishment, in a way that is balanced for our bodies, as well as being mindful of the need to maintain sustainable food production systems for the future. That means eating seasonally, locally and organically. These recipes have all been designed with this in mind: eating in harmony with nature, with joy, but without waste.

RECIPES Adam Caisley, Gaven Fuller, Katriona Jones and Lydia Lishman
PHOTOGRAPHY Lizzie Mayson FOOD STYLING Frankie Unsworth PROP STYLING Linda Berlin

Spiced butternut and lentil soup

with a kale pesto swirl and toasted English cobnut and seed crumble

SERVES 2-4

1 tbsp coconut oil
1 medium onion, peeled
  and chopped
1 celery stick, chopped
600g butternut squash,
  peeled and chopped
  into 2.5cm cubes
1 garlic clove, chopped
a thumb-sized piece
  of ginger, peeled
  and grated
a 2.5cm piece of fresh
  turmeric, grated
½ medium red chilli,
  finely chopped
1 tsp ground cumin
1 tsp ground coriander
200g red lentils
1 litre fresh vegetable
  or chicken stock
sea salt and black
  pepper
100ml natural yoghurt,
  to serve

FOR THE KALE PESTO

100g pumpkin seeds
100g kale
200ml extra virgin olive oil
2 garlic cloves
juice of 1 lemon
½ tsp clear honey

FOR THE COBNUT
AND SEED CRUMBLE

50g cobnuts, shelled
50g pumpkin seeds

METHOD

Heat the coconut oil in a large saucepan over a medium heat and add the onion and celery. Fry gently for 5 minutes until the onion has softened and is translucent. Add the butternut squash and continue to cook for a further 5 minutes, stirring to make sure the vegetables don't stick to the bottom of the pan.

Preheat the oven to 180°C.

Add the garlic, ginger, turmeric, chilli and ground spices and stir over the heat for 1 minute. Stir in the red lentils, quickly followed by the stock. Bring to the boil then lower the heat and simmer gently for 15–20 minutes until the lentils are cooked and the cubes of squash break easily under the back of a fork. Season with salt and pepper and blend well to a smooth, velvety consistency. Taste the soup and adjust the seasoning if needed.

Put the pumpkin seeds for the pesto on a small baking tray and the cobnuts and pumpkin seeds for the crumble on a separate tray. Place both trays in the oven for 10–12 minutes, or until the nuts and seeds are golden. Once toasted, tip the tray with the cobnuts into a pestle and mortar with a pinch of salt and crush until you have a coarse crumble; set the tray of plain pumpkin seeds aside.

Bring a large pan of salted water to the boil and blanch the kale for 1 minute. Drain and plunge into iced water straight away. Then drain again, squeezing out as much water as you can. Transfer the kale to a blender with the remaining pesto ingredients and the toasted pumpkin seeds and blend to a coarse paste. Taste and add a little more salt, pepper, lemon or honey as needed.

To serve, spoon the soup into warm bowls and top with a swirl of yoghurt, a little pesto and finally the toasted crumbled cobnuts and pumpkin seeds.

Any leftover pesto can be stored in a jar, covered with a thin layer of oil, for up to a week.

This soup is very gently spiced, giving it a hint of warmth and fragrance, which is complemented by the earthy kale pesto and the crunch of the cobnut and seed topping.

We've suggested using butternut squash but other varieties, such as Crown Prince, Golden Hubbard and Harlequin are all good substitutes. The leftover pesto is ideal for creating a meal later in the week, either stirred through pasta or gnocchi, or loosened with a little olive oil and used as a salad dressing.

Warm roasted squash and blue cheese salad
with black turtle beans, wild rice and rocket

SERVES 4

225g dried black turtle
  beans, soaked
  in water overnight
125g wild rice, rinsed
  in cold water
425g butternut squash,
  cut into wedges
4 tsp olive oil
60g rocket, roughly
  chopped
½ red chilli, finely diced
2 tsp lemon juice
160g blue cheese,
  such as Daylesford
  blue, crumbled
sea salt and black
  pepper

FOR THE HONEY DRESSING

1 tsp Dijon mustard
2 tsp wholegrain
  mustard
2 tsp cider vinegar
1–2 tsp clear honey
2 tbsp olive oil

METHOD

Rinse the beans, place in a large saucepan and cover with cold water by about 2.5cm. Bring to the boil and cook the beans until tender, about 10–15 minutes. Drain in a colander and leave the beans to steam dry.

Put the rice into a medium saucepan, cover with cold water and bring to the boil then simmer until tender, about 20 minutes.

Preheat the oven to 200°C fan.

For the dressing, in a small bowl whisk the mustards, cider vinegar and honey together then gradually add the oil.

Place the squash on a baking tray, drizzle with the olive oil, add a little seasoning and roast until tender, about 20–30 minutes. Transfer to a large mixing bowl add the rocket, chilli and lemon juice, toss with the dressing then check the seasoning. Place in a serving bowl and crumble over the blue cheese. Serve immediately.

Squash, apple and walnut muffins
with a crunchy oat topping

MAKES 6

100g walnuts
100g muscovado sugar
150ml olive oil
50ml natural yoghurt
2 large eggs
150g self-raising flour
1 tsp baking powder
1 tsp mixed sweet spice
1 tsp ground cinnamon

pinch of sea salt
50g rolled oats, plus
    extra to sprinkle
100g butternut squash,
    peeled and grated
100g apple,
    peeled and grated
2 tbsp maple syrup

Inspired by
the flavours of
a traditional
carrot cake, these
vegetable-based
muffins are made
with little sugar
and wholesome
oats. They don't
taste very sweet,
so are suitable for
breakfast as well
as an afternoon
snack. You can also
leave out the apple
and increase the
quantity of squash
for more of a
savoury muffin.

METHOD

Preheat the oven to 180°C. Line six holes of a deep muffin tray with cases or squares of parchment paper.

Place the walnuts on a baking tray and toast in the oven for 10–12 minutes or until golden. Remove and roughly chop.

Combine the sugar, olive oil, yoghurt and eggs in a large bowl and beat until thoroughly combined.

Into a separate bowl, sift the flour, baking powder, spices and salt. Tip this into the wet mixture and stir to combine evenly. Next stir in the oats, squash and apple and 80g of the walnuts, keeping the remainder to one side.

Divide the batter between the muffin cases and sprinkle the top of each muffin with the remaining walnuts and a scattering of oats. Drizzle over the maple syrup and bake in the centre of the oven for 20–25 minutes until well risen and springy to touch.

Place the muffins on a wire rack to cool. Either serve warm or once cool, store in an airtight tin for up to 3 days.

This broth has a deep, rich flavour and is both nourishing and sustaining. It is a good source of vitamin D and beta glucan which support immunity and gut health and are useful in balancing blood sugar.

Mushroom broth
with kimchi

**SERVES 2
AS MAIN COURSE,
4 AS A SNACK
OR STARTER**

20g dried porcini
   mushrooms
20g dried mixed
   mushrooms
500ml warm water
1 litre good-quality
   vegetable stock or
   white chicken stock
2 tbsp white miso paste
5 chestnut mushrooms,
   thinly sliced
20g enoki mushrooms
1 dried kombu leaf
5g ginger, peeled
   and cut into thin
   matchsticks
10g spring onion,
   trimmed and cut
   into thin matchsticks
2–4 tbsp kimchi
coriander sprigs, to
   garnish

METHOD

Rehydrate the dried mushrooms by placing them in a small bowl with the warm water.

In a medium saucepan, heat the stock, add the miso paste and bring to the boil, then remove from the heat and leave to stand for 5 minutes before passing through a strainer. Return the stock to the pan and bring to a gentle simmer, then add the rehydrated mushrooms and their steeping water. Add the chestnut and enoki mushrooms, kombu leaf, ginger and spring onion and allow to simmer for 1 minute.

To serve, spoon the kimchi into the base of each serving bowl before pouring over the broth, adding any cooked soba noodles, tofu or leftover cooked chicken if you want to make it more of a substantial meal, and garnishing with the coriander.

Partridge, kale and chanterelles
with Cheddar mash

SERVES 6

8 skinned breasts
    and legs of partridge
plain flour, for coating
olive oil
2 medium onions,
    peeled and diced
1 garlic clove, chopped
3 thyme sprigs
300ml white wine
1 litre good-quality
    brown chicken stock
1 celeriac (about 500g),
    peeled and cut into
    2.5cm pieces
3 medium carrots,
    peeled and diced
3 celery sticks,
    peeled and diced
handful of flat-leaf
    parsley, chopped
sea salt and black
    pepper

FOR THE KALE AND CHANTERELLES
200g kale
100g chanterelle
    mushrooms
knob of unsalted butter

FOR THE CHEDDAR MASH
1.2kg floury potatoes,
    peeled and halved
300g unsalted butter
4 garlic cloves,
    finely chopped
200g Cheddar, grated
pinch of ground nutmeg

METHOD

For the mash, add the potatoes to a large saucepan of simmering salted water and cook until soft, about 15–20 minutes. Drain and mash, then beat in the butter and garlic and fold in the Cheddar and nutmeg. Check for seasoning before serving.

Meanwhile, season the partridge breasts and legs with salt and pepper. Put the flour in a shallow bowl and roll the partridge pieces in it to coat. Place a large casserole over a high heat with a drizzle of oil. Add the partridge and seal the meat until golden brown all over. Remove from the casserole and set to one side.

Add a drizzle more oil to the casserole, then add the onions and garlic, turn the heat to medium, cover with a lid and leave them to sweat for a few minutes until they start to soften, then add the thyme then the white wine.

Bring the wine to a simmer and leave it, uncovered, to reduce by half, then add the chicken stock and the rest of the vegetables, and bring the liquid back to a simmer. Cook for a further 5 minutes, then add the partridge and continue to cook for a further 5 minutes.

Wash the kale and add it to a pan with just the water clinging to its leaves. Cover and cook over a medium heat until just wilted, about 3 minutes.

Meanwhile, melt the butter in a frying pan and fry the mushrooms over a medium–high heat, until soft all the way through and browned. Fold through the kale.

Serve the partridge with the kale and chanterelles and the mash alongside.

Eating wild game is arguably more sustainable than buying intensively-farmed meat, but you do need to ask questions about its provenance. There is a difference between truly wild game and managed animals that are reared for sport.

Partridge is a good introduction to game: it is lean, with a milder, sweeter flavour than other wild birds. It pairs well with its seasonal companions; earthy autumnal vegetables such as kale and wild mushrooms. Your butcher will joint and prepare it for you.

Baked Penyston Brie
with honey and truffle

At Daylesford, the dairy is the seed from which the farm has grown. And as with any traditional farmshop, the organic milk, butter, cheeses and yoghurts remain at its heart.

A small team develops, matures and moulds 10 different cheeses, Penyston Brie being the newest. The nature of organic milk means that it changes throughout the year, so the cheesemakers must understand and work in harmony with its natural properties. And like all seasonal produce, there are times of the year when cheeses are at their best.

Penyston Brie is a mild and creamy cheese that is ripened for at least five weeks to create an earthy, almost mushroom-like flavour that pairs beautifully with truffle. It is at its most interesting in the cold months, when the cattle's rich winter milk gives the cheese an even more buttery taste and texture. Camembert is a good alternative.

SERVES 4

1 small Daylesford Penyston
    Brie or 1 small Camembert
10g fresh truffle
2 tsp clear honey

TO SERVE

crusty sourdough bread
vegetable crudités,
    such as baby carrots,
    celery, cauliflower,
    purple sprouting
    broccoli, radishes

METHOD

Preheat the oven to 170°C fan.

Place the Penyston Brie in a small ovenproof dish and bake in the oven for 8–10 minutes, until the cheese has softened, and the centre is soft and gooey.

Cut a hole out of the centre of the top of the cheese, carefully lift back the skin.

Finely grate the truffle into the centre then drizzle over the honey. Serve with crusty sourdough bread or toast and a selection of vegetables crudités.

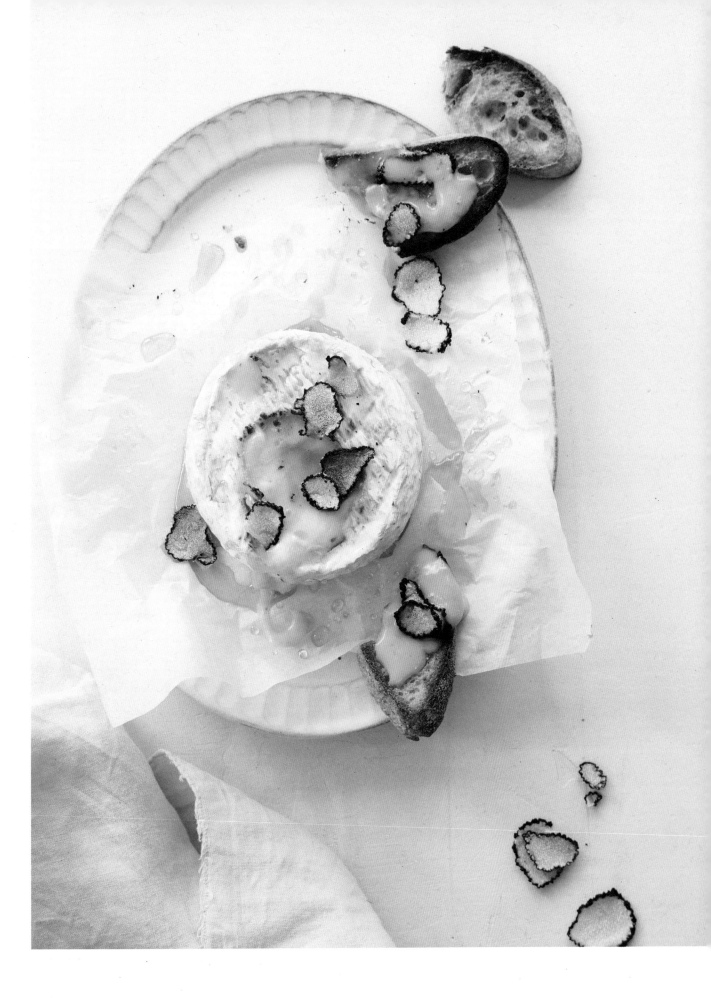

Apple and hedgerow jelly

MAKES 6 X 200ML JARS

1.4kg crab apples
    or cooking apples,
    such as Bramley
700g wild blackberries
    (or a mixture of rowan
    berries, damsons,
    rosehips to make up
    the same quantity)
1.2 litres water
granulated sugar

METHOD

Wash the fruit. Remove the stalks from the apples and if using cooking apples chop into quarters. Place the apples and berries in a preserving pan and cover with water. Cook on a gentle heat for 20–30 minutes, until the fruit has softened and become pulpy.

Place a muslin jelly bag over a clean bowl and pour in the fruit pulp. Allow the bag to hang over the bowl and leave to strain overnight. Avoid squeezing the bag as the jelly will become cloudy.

The next day, measure the extracted liquid. For every 600ml of juice add 450g of sugar.

In the preserving pan, gently heat the juice and sugar, stirring occasionally. Once the sugar has dissolved, increase the heat and bring to a rolling boil for approximately 10 minutes until the setting point has been reached. To test it, add a teaspoon of liquid to a cold plate and return the plate to the fridge for 2 minutes. The jelly has set when running your finger through the jam leaves a crinkle. If it has not set, continue to boil and test again. Skim carefully to remove any impurities.

Pour into sterilised jars, cover and store in a cool dry cupboard. Once opened, the jelly can be kept in the fridge for up to 5 days.

As the autumn progresses, the British hedgerows come alive with deep crimson and purple berries and these are a free and sustainable source of food, provided we respect them and collect responsibly.

Wild food is very important for the survival of the UK's wildlife so we need to forage with care to ensure there is enough left for birds and others. Autumn is a time for harvesting but also for storing and preserving that harvest, and making jams and jellies is a wonderful way to use up seasonal gluts of fruit.

Apple and blackberry Charlotte
with a spiced glaze

SERVES 4

420g cooking apples
(Bramleys work well)
120g blackberries
grated zest and juice
of ½ lemon
90–100g caster sugar,
depending on how
tart the fruits are
110g unsalted butter,
melted, plus some
softened butter to
grease the moulds
12 slices of leftover bread,
medium thickness,
crusts removed

FOR THE SPICED GLAZE

60g caster sugar
pinch of ground
cinnamon
very small pinch
of ground clove

TO SERVE

English custard
or crème fraîche

METHOD

Put four dariole moulds into the fridge to chill for at least 1 hour.

Peel, core and roughly chop the apples, place in a large pan on a medium heat, then add the blackberries and bring to the boil with a tablespoon of water, the lemon juice and zest and sugar and cook until the apple starts to break down but still has some lumps in it. Set aside and allow to cool.

Preheat the oven to 170ºC fan.

Mix the glaze ingredients together in a small bowl until well combined. Butter the insides of the moulds then pour the spiced sugar mixture into a mould and turn it to coat the surface, then empty the sugar into another mould and repeat; continue to do this until all moulds are coated with the spiced sugar.

Cut the bread into 4 discs for the base of the moulds and 4 slightly larger discs for the top, then cut the remainder into fingers. Brush all the bread shapes with the melted butter on one side. Place the smaller disc, butter-side down, in the base of each mould then position the fingers around the sides of the mould (again butter-side down) with each piece slightly overlapping, then spoon in the apple mix. Close the top with the slightly larger disc of buttered bread, butter-side up, and fold over any bread from the sides to form a seal.

Place on a baking tray and bake in the oven for 40 minutes or until the lids are golden and crisp, then remove and allow to set for 5 minutes before turning the Charlottes on to serving plates. Let them sit for a least another 5 minutes before lifting the mould away. Serve with custard or crème fraîche.

Quince sorbet
with oat crumble

SERVES 4

4 medium quince,
    cut into wedges
375ml dry white wine
350g caster sugar
1 vanilla pod, split
400ml water
juice of ½ lemon

FOR THE OAT CRUMBLE

140g unsalted butter,
    from the fridge,
    diced
140g plain flour
large pinch of ground
    cinnamon
100g soft light
    brown sugar
150g rolled oats

METHOD

Rub the fur off the quince and place them in a large stockpot. Add the wine, sugar and vanilla pod and cover the pot with a tight-fitting lid. Bring the liquid to a boil and leave to simmer gently for 3–3½ hours. Push the mix through a fine sieve, collecting it in a clean bowl.

Stir in the water and the lemon juice, then churn in an ice-cream machine according to the manufacturer's instructions.

Preheat the oven to 180°C.

To make the crumble, place all the ingredients except the oats in a food processor and pulse until the mixture resembles fine breadcrumbs, then stir in the oats. Place on a large baking tray and bake in the oven for 12 minutes until golden brown. Remove from the oven and allow to cool.

Serve the sorbet in bowls with the oat crumble sprinkled over the top. Store any leftover crumble in an airtight jar for up to 2 weeks.

SEEDS OF FREEDOM

WORDS Satish Kumar ILLUSTRATION Hugo Guinness

Once an Indian sage asked his student to go and find the smallest seed on earth. The student went into the forest, examining seeds of all kinds. He eventually came to a banyan tree and found a fig full of many seeds. He picked one of them, returned to the sage and said, 'this is the smallest seed that I could find. It is so small that I can hardly see it. I need a magnifying glass!'

The sage said, 'this is a fine seed. Can you crush it?'

'Yes, I can,' said the student.

'What is inside it?' asked the sage.

'I can see nothing inside it,' answered the student.

'This smallest seed, smaller than all seeds, contains one of the largest trees in the world – the banyan tree, the tree of a thousand branches, nourishing, maintaining and nurturing all kinds of life, and producing fruits full of seeds to create more trees. It is this small seed

which is the basis of the tree of life and the tree of knowledge. Meditate on this seed and you will be enlightened.' The sage continued, 'the Buddha sat under a banyan tree and was enlightened.'

'Do you mean to say that I should meditate on the seed rather than on the mantra Om?' asked the student.

'Om itself is a seed. We call it a seed mantra. The banyan seed, as all seeds, contains the dream of the universe. Can you count and contemplate the number of trees in a single banyan seed? This one seed represents eternity,' said the sage. 'A seed produces a tree, a tree produces seed. This is the eternal cycle.'

In all ancient cultures the seed is sacred. Farmers harvest their crops but in their wisdom, first they save the seeds for the next year and only then will they celebrate the harvest and feast on the nourishing food. Saving their own seeds gives them food sovereignty, food freedom, self-respect, dignity and self-

reliance. For them the story of food and farming and the story of life are written in the story of seeds.

In our modern time, dominated by materialism, the sense of the sacred has been lost. Seeds have become mere commodities and as a consequence thousands of varieties of traditional and local seeds have disappeared. Agriculture has become agri-business. For industrial farmers, who have turned agriculture into monoculture, food and seeds are simply a resource for making money, whereas for ecological farmers, who grow food to feed people, agriculture is a source of life. For them, farming is a way of living well by caring for the soil and caring for the natural world.

More and more people are experiencing the negative effects of food grown with genetically-engineered seeds or with chemical fertilisers and pesticides. Citizens around the world can see that despite the increasing quantity of food in supermarkets the nutritional quality of food has diminished. Large numbers

'The desire to save seeds
comes from an ethical urge
to defend life's evolution.'

–Vandana Shiva,
founder of the Navdanya organisation which
promotes biodiversity conservation

of people are suffering from obesity, food allergies, depression and other forms of disease, due to fake food. Real food can only come from real seeds so protecting the integrity and diversity of seeds, soil and farming is imperative. Seeds that are adapted to their local climate are strong and healthy and they ensure the health of the people and the health of planet Earth. Seeds are the commons of humanity yet today they are monopolised by four or five giant corporations – that cannot be a true free market. Seed freedom must be recognised as an integral part of human freedom and patenting seeds needs to be avoided at all costs.

Modern methods of farming have disconnected many farmers from the land. They no longer farm. They don't touch the soil. There is an absence of animal husbandry. Mega machines, huge tractors, combine harvesters, lifeless robots and complicated computers run the process of food production. Tender, loving care of the soil, of the seeds and the plants and animals is a forgotten dream. The majority of farmers have been turned into technicians, machine minders and computer operators. This is a tragedy inflicted upon people in the name of progress, development, economic growth and high living standards. And in addition to the ill health suffered by many people, it is becoming clear that industrial farming has a huge negative impact on the health of the land and the soil. Food systems dependent on artificial fertilisers put enormous stress on the environment by producing pollution, waste and greenhouse gases which contribute to the climate crisis.

In the wake of this depressing story a few courageous and enlightened farmers are standing up for the rights of the genuine growers and seed savers of our time. They are the champions of agroecology, organic farming, permaculture and seed banks. These seed banks distribute traditional seeds free of charge. Like air, water and sunshine, seeds should be free for all. These farmers are the voices of sanity and wisdom. True scientists, their cause is rooted in respect for nature, for seed diversity, biodiversity, sustainability and evolutionary principles. Science of this kind works in harmony with ethics and ecology.

The constructive and practical work of agroecology and seed banks shows that campaigning against the genetic modification of seeds is complemented by the positive action of learning and living in harmony with the soil and the seeds. That is the way to sustain our economy and our culture.

For climate stability, for environmental sustainability, for food security and human survival we need to safeguard the soil and the seeds. This is ancient wisdom and common sense. That is the lesson from the Indian sage who saw eternity in a banyan seed; we may be able to count the number of seeds on a banyan tree but we cannot count the number of banyan trees in a seed.

Satish Kumar is the author of Soil, Soul & Society *and* Elegant Simplicity *and Editor Emeritus for* Resurgence & Ecologist *magazine.*

44

breathing —
the poetry of
the air

exhaling —
finding peace
in who I am

choosing freedom
in every breath
I inhale

open
to your breath
— trust it

let breath
be your guide
— rest easy

slow down
go quietly
— breathe

inhale —
life's sweet perfume
breathe and live it

breath of life
flows in this body
— I am rich

simply breathing —
everything comes
and goes

exhaling deeply —
as water washes stone
breath sweeps mind

ANDO

'Breathing creates the platform on which everything else – health, happiness, cognitive ability, elevated performance, success and influence – is built.'

–Dr Alan Watkins, founder and CEO of Complete Coherence Ltd

BREATH WORKS
WHY WE ALL NEED TO EXHALE MORE

In the 1990s, I was an alcoholic working in advertising. I was very productive but at a great cost, to myself and others. I was stressed, depressed and not coping well. Following the sudden and tragic death of my brother in 1998, I realised that my life needed to change. So I went from the out-of-control world of obsessive doing to the seemingly calmer waters of life as a yoga and meditation teacher – a life of being. I learned that by controlling my breath, I could control my mind. By strengthening and opening my body, I could find increased mental clarity and emotional resilience. And then I started to create and do again, this time from a place of stillness. Rather than seeing 'being' and 'doing' as opposites, I realised they were in fact two sides of one coin.

I like to call this integration, 'well-doing'. And at its heart is a connection to our breath. Living well in our busy lives needs growing self-awareness and the ability to cope with sudden change and recover from being overloaded. By making our breath our constant companion, we have an inner coach that can help us calm our minds, find focus and then rest and recover, whenever we need it.

Thousands of years ago the yogis of India also looked to understand their minds and bodies better by looking within. Key to this process of self-understanding was the science of *pranayama* – using breathing exercises as a means of controlling the flow of energy in the mind–body system. By mastering their breath, yogis learnt to tone and control their bodies and manage their mental and emotional states better. It's difficult to breathe slowly and think too much at the same time.

In so many yoga classes most of the time is spent on the physical side to the practice, but in fact, the most advanced practices of yoga are the disciplines that focus on breathing and meditation rather than movement and postures. It's an integrated discipline that works best when there is a balance of breathing, relaxation and meditation, along with the physical exercise.

WORDS Michael Townsend Williams
PHOTOGRAPHY Jim Marsden

With the global rise in popularity of wellness, yoga and mindfulness, breathing practitioners are becoming the latest stars. However, breathing is also emerging as a means of helping people in so many other parts of life. Slow, controlled breathing is recommended by doctors for managing anxiety. New products that help guide your breathing have been approved by health authorities in the US and the UK to help lower blood pressure. Children are learning how to breathe from their bellies as part of mindfulness in school programmes aimed at reducing stress in children as young as five. Men and women from the emergency services are trained in breathing to cope with trauma. Actors deal with stage fright by breathing from their diaphragms. Sports stars learn how to focus under pressure by bringing their breath under control first.

There is also an array of innovative products to help you breathe better: gadgets that shine a rhythmic light onto your bedroom ceiling to breathe yourself to sleep; ways to purify your air at home; apps that measure your breathing and train you to breathe better, like my own, Do Breathe.

Yet, with all the excitement around the possibilities of breathing better I am continually amazed by how few of us actually do breathe in a healthy way every day. Most of us breathe too quickly, taking around 15–20 breaths per minute, as opposed to the more natural, slower rhythm of 10–12. We then compound the problem when we overreact to life's niggles by breathing in more, often from the chest and through the mouth rather than the nose, which exaggerates the stress response, uses more energy and gives us less control. Without even realising it, we are using our breath in stressful situations – to make things worse. The simple remedy is to re-learn how we were born to breathe, which I've distilled into three simple steps (see opposite). If you want to make the most of your lesser-known superpower – your own breath – begin with this simple guide.

Breathe well. Be well. Do well.

Michael Townsend Williams is the author and co-founder of Do Breathe, *www.dobreathe.com*

BREATHE WELL

There are many techniques from both the East and the West that teach us how to breathe in a way that is best for our well-being. The basics, however, are simple and actually the most important for everyday use. As well as following the advice below, see if you can slow down your breathing to around 10–12 breaths per minute. Once that feels okay try breathing in for four and out for six, which brings it down to six breaths per minute – the optimal rate if you really want to relax your nervous system.

1. Breathe in and out from the belly
Breathing from the belly you feel more centred and more in control. This diaphragmatic or abdominal breathing (I prefer to say 'belly') is efficient and, once established, easy and natural.

2. Breathe in and out through the nose
(rather than the mouth)
The nose is designed for breathing. The little hairs in the nostrils filter out particles in the air. The chamber behind the nose cools or warms the air to within one degree of the body's temperature. Except for certain situations like high-intensity sport, your nose does a much better job of breathing than your mouth.

3. Breathe out a little more than you breathe in
Exhaling is linked to the body's relaxation response as it stimulates the parasympathetic branch of the autonomic nervous system. Once you're in balance you can breathe in and out equally. But in my experience most of us are so frequently stressed that a little more exhalation with every breath is a good idea.

10 REASONS TO BREATHE BETTER

1. Lowered stress
Slow, controlled breathing lowers your heart rate, relaxes your muscles and dampens the stress response.

2. Improved health
Breathing not only improves your mental health but also can be used to lower blood pressure.

3. Enhanced brain function
Nasal breathing has been shown to improve the cognitive performance of the brain.

4. Conscious behaviour
Awareness of your breathing gives you the ability to respond to life rather than react to it, and make better decisions.

5. Working better
Increasing the well-being of employees leads to better business performance. And key to this is managing your energy levels and your emotions. Luckily, breathing can help you do both.

6. Relating well
Listening to others, having empathy and learning to relate well are all influenced by the ability to use breathing to manage emotions and have healthy relationships.

7. Increased confidence
Leaning into difficult areas of your life is challenging and stressful. So much so that often we avoid them. Breathing slowly and deeply can help you push through some of these tricky moments, building resilience, courage and confidence on the way.

8. More clarity
In the complex lives we lead, learning to pause and reflect and gain perspective is an essential tool to ensure we are clear about what really matters to us. Awareness of your breath brings your attention from your thoughts to your feelings, creating mental space.

9. Communicating well
Becoming more aware of the breath and your feelings you also become more attuned to the feelings of others. Saying less and meaning more comes more naturally.

10. Controlling your attention
Whatever your intention, if you can't control your attention then you won't be able to control the direction of your life. More and more companies and technologies are vying for our attention, we all have a simple choice to make: learn the art of self-control or be controlled more by others.

THE NEW
NATURALS

WORDS Francesca White
ILLUSTRATION Blandine Pannequin

If you scanned the beauty shelves 10 years ago for 'natural' skincare (a blanket term, which encompassed everything from organic to botanical to those ranges suitable for sensitive skin) the pickings weren't slim – but they were slightly underwhelming. Not because they were not beautifully-packaged, or eco-friendly or pleasantly-scented – but because they didn't deliver results.

Yes, we all want a product that calms, softens and makes our skin look lovely and plump. But after that initial glow has worn off, when early mornings and sleepless nights and hours spent in the blue-light glare of a computer have started to take their toll, we suddenly need our moisturiser to work a little harder. This is where the 'new naturals' come in.

The next-generation skincare that you'll find on the shelves (or in the spa or online) is still packed with all of nature's most revered skin-soothers (like rose, good for intense nourishment, or aloe vera, renowned for its healing, hydrating abilities). But in these products is also where you'll find some supercharged ingredients in hiding. Referred to as 'actives', these potent ingredients have been cleverly formulated into cleansers, oils, serums and creams – and suddenly, naturals are being acknowledged as serious contenders in the skincare industry.

Currently enjoying immense hype (and for good reason) is the humble rosehip. Rich in Vitamin A (otherwise known as retinol – an antioxidant renowned for its regenerative, wrinkle-reducing properties), rosehip seed oil is proven to fade fine lines and scars while spurring skin cell regeneration. Long used in pregnancy (it's excellent on stretch marks) it restores elasticity and spring to the skin.

Then there's liquorice. An excellent skin-brightener, liquorice root extract is rich in an antioxidant called glabridin and licochalcone A, both of which help to smooth the tone and texture of the skin. Thanks to its brightening properties, liquorice root has found its way into several skincare products, such as pigmentation-reducing serums and dark circle-erasing eye creams. Unlike its chemical equivalent, hydroquinone (a powerful lightening agent, which still comes under scrutiny for its potentially dangerous side effects), it's safe to use – even in the sun.

But what about exfoliants? How do these new naturals compare to the glycolics, the lactics and the salicylics, long-regarded as the surefire route to a radiant complexion? Fruit-derived AHAs (alpha hydroxy acids) might be the answer. Rich in enzymes, which gently dissolve dead skin cells, these naturally-occurring acids boast the same skin-resurfacing properties as their chemical counterparts, minus the irritation. They're found in pineapples, lemons, apples and grapes. A glowing, fresher-looking face awaits.

These supercharged ingredients aren't simply a way to nourish skin naturally – they're a solution for sensitivity and some of today's most persistent inflammatory conditions. Green tea is said to help reduce rosacea (often treated with azelaic acid; not always well-tolerated); pine bark extract claims to calm psoriasis (far nicer than aggressive steroid creams). And whether it's stress or synthetic ingredients that are causing breakouts, natural clays and tea tree oils can help to draw out impurities naturally (and won't strip the skin like sulphur-based solutions).

Happily, today's high-performance complexion-perfectors are easy to identify, thanks to simple-to-read labels and brands' integrity about highlighting the ingredients inside their bottles. In doing so, these new naturals are also informing modern consumers, and inspiring them to take a conscious role when it comes to deciding what goes on their faces. After all, knowledge is power – and when the oils, the essences and the extracts in your skincare are this exciting, why hide them?

TULIPS

HOW TO SELECT, PLANT AND MAKE THE MOST
OF THESE POPULAR SPRING BULBS

WORDS Jez Taylor PHOTOGRAPHY Lizzie Mayson

Tulips kick off the cut-flower season in a kaleidoscope of colour and form, going far beyond the comparatively limited palette of the slightly earlier narcissi.

WHERE TO BEGIN?

Tulip bulb companies are generally based in Holland or have strong Dutch associations. All have very accessible online catalogues declaring the awesomeness of each variety. My advice would be not to go with the cheapest source; I have in the past and have regretted it. As a rule, the bigger the bulb the better the bloom – buying smaller bulbs of the more expensive varieties is a waste of money if you get no bloom at all.

WHICH BULBS TO CHOOSE?

There are early, mid- or late-flowering types, or there are form types; paeony-like, fringed, parrot, lily-flowered, green or some unusual niche species for geeks who like multi-flowered clumps of 10cm-high tulips on their rockery. I would suggest choosing a range that will flower across the season. I have suffered with early varieties and frost in the past couple of years, so the earlies make up only about 15 per cent of my selection. I think it's always good to have a strong quota of late-flowering varieties because even if it is hot in April, the later types will extend the season by at least 10 days. Other than that, if you have spaces to fill, then indulge and choose a dozen beautiful varieties from the bulb catalogues.

PLANTING

Delaying planting until late October reduces the risk of the fungal disease 'tulip fire', which thrives in warm conditions and can devastate crops. In the garden at Daylesford, we plant about 8–10cm deep; deep enough for the flowering stem to maintain a stable upright state when in heavy bloom. If you want to establish tulips permanently in a border then you must choose your variety with care – some will only perform if lifted, dried and replanted each autumn. You will need to plant the bulbs deeper, at 15–20cm. If you plant too shallow then tulips have a tendency to multiply into a cluster of small bulbs, which don't have the strength to throw a bloom.

If you are going to make the effort, then choose a well-observed location where the tulips will bring strong colour and cheer; they make a great spread among other perennial plantings that bring colour later on in the season.

MY FAVOURITES

Of the 50 or so varieties I have grown at Daylesford over the past two years, opposite are some of my favourites; these have performed well for me here.

SPRING GREEN
has green and ivory striped flowers.

WHITE TRIUMPHATOR
has a classic lily-flowered shape and a pure white colour; it's great in mixed arrangements.

ELEGANT LADY
is another lily-flowered variety with tall flowers edged with pale mauve.

GREENLAND
has striking wide pink leaves with striped green spines.

JAMES LAST
has delicate, slightly twisted petals, and is an unusual lilac colour.
(pictured left)

Jez Taylor has been managing the Market Garden at Daylesford Farm since 2008. He grows over 500 varieties of fruit and vegetable organically as well as a range of cut flowers. Jez makes cider in his spare time.

HOW TO REDUCE YOUR FOOD WASTE

WORDS Katriona Jones PHOTOGRAPHY Lizzie Mayson

1

WRITE A WEEKLY MEAL PLAN

and abide by it when you shop. Make your choices based on what you already have in the fridge or cupboards and what's in season – this will mean you use up old ingredients first as well as save money.

2

DON'T DISCARD YOUR STALE BREAD

It is the most wasted product in the UK, with 24 million slices thrown away every day, but there are plenty of ways to make use of what isn't fit for your sandwiches. Make breadcrumbs by whizzing stale slices in a food processor or blender. Lightly fry cubes in oil to make croutons and store them in jars for up to 2 weeks. Look up recipes that make use of stale bread, such as bread and butter pudding or a panzanella salad. The apple and blackberry Charlotte recipe on page 39 is perfect for combining your stale loaf with a glut of fruit.

3

USE THE WHOLE PLANT

Broccoli and cauliflower stalks can be cooked along with the rest of the vegetable or used in soups, mash or purées. Beetroot leaves are delicious in salads or cooked as you would spinach. Add carrot tops to pesto or salsas; leftover vegetable ends and peelings to stocks; and chopped herb stalks to soups.

4

KEEP A SMALL COMPOST BIN

in your kitchen and use it for food scraps, egg shells and wilted fruits and vegetables. Depending on where you live and whether you have a garden you can either keep a compost pile outside or your council will collect your bags.

Throwing away a carrot that's past its best or the remnants of the pot of pasta we didn't quite finish might seem like a harmless act but the consequences of discarding food are far-reaching. Wasted food is one of the world's largest contributors to climate change and the statistics are stark: UK households throw away more than 7 million tons of food every year and at least 400,000 tons of it could have been redistributed to feed those in need.

Approximately a third of the food produced for global human consumption is lost or wasted each year, while nearly 800 million people suffer from chronic malnourishment. Food waste is a very grave issue but it is something we can each help tackle. There are small but simple steps and preventative measures we can all take to minimise (and eliminate) our waste.

5

SOUPS, STEWS, RISOTTOS AND DHALS

are all fantastic ways to use up tired vegetables, leftover meat or pulses, dairy products such as crème fraîche or yoghurt and even those half-empty packets at the back of your cupboards.

6

HAVE CONFIDENCE IN YOUR OWN JUDGEMENT OVER EXPIRY DATES

Knowing what is meant by 'best-before' and 'use-by' could mean the difference between turning the contents of your fridge into a meal and throwing away perfectly edible food. Stored correctly, good-quality, fresh produce can last longer than you think. The use-by dates are merely a guide so use your own sense of sight, smell and taste to judge whether something should be thrown away.

7

FREEZE

Leftovers, soups, sauces and bread are all obvious contenders for freezing, but even ingredients such as egg whites can be frozen for up to 12 months. Grated hard cheese can be stored in small boxes. Chopped onions, herbs, berries, garlic, ginger or chillies all keep well in the freezer and are great to have on hand when you're cooking. Fruit can be blended into smoothies and frozen in ice-cube trays, and even pesto is perfect for freezing.

8

STORE WISELY

How you store your food can increase its shelf life by days, weeks and even months. Treat greens such as kale, chard, fresh herbs, sprouting broccoli or asparagus as you would a bunch of flowers: trim the ends and store upright in a glass or jar of water. You will find they retain colour, freshness and crunch for 2–3 days longer this way. Not all fruit and veg should be stored in the fridge; most root veg and alliums prefer a slightly less cool temperature and to be kept away from direct sunlight.

SHIFTING TIDES

WORDS Imogen Fortes
PHOTOGRAPHY Helen Cathcart

It's a sunny, clear morning as I make my way along one of southeast London's arterial thoroughfares to meet Celia Dowson. Passing Camberwell Arts School, I leave the traffic fumes and urban throb behind me as I turn into Vanguard Court, a quiet, cobbled cul-de-sac, home to a vibrant community of artists and artisans. The low-ceilinged, bright, but compact studio Celia shares with fellow graduates from the Royal College of Art, feels like a fitting but also a slightly curious choice of workplace for an artist whose work is so heavily informed by wide, expansive spaces and the movement and flux in nature.

'There's a feeling of camaraderie and community here – a like-mindedness – so it's an inspiring place for someone like me who is still quite fresh out of art school,' she tells me. 'And while my design process begins with a concept – walking, or gathering things from a particular landscape, to try and develop an idea in my mind, the process of bringing it to life is very technical and this space suits that side to my work.'

Celia's milky-white porcelain vessels streaked with sweeping black marks are inspired by the Gower Peninsula in Wales. 'I visit the area often because I have family there. Rhossili Bay is this vast headland that juts out into a wild and changeable sea and I wanted to draw out the qualities of the landscape. There is a huge tidal shift, so the pieces reflect that turbulence and movement; to me they look like crashing waves but they're also very abstract. People see different things in them and that's what I'm hoping for. You don't need to know my story to enjoy a piece; I want it to evoke something in you so that it will give meaning to your life.'

That study of space is a theme that reoccurs in Celia's work. To write the dissertation for her MA she spent time in India studying, observing, meditating and practising yoga, which led her to consider the different ways we understand and interpret space: architectural, internal–external, mind and body, immersive space, and the differing Eastern and Western perspectives of it. 'I enjoy being quiet and

contemplative – finding space in my own mind. I love yoga and am fascinated by Eastern philosophy, so that element of my work is very personal.'

Like many contemporary artists, Celia is interested in how technology and its advances can interact with the artist's hand. She dismissively describes herself as a 'geek' who enjoys the technical side to her work, but one gets the sense that there is a certain pride in the depiction, a knowledge that this is what sets her apart from many of her contemporaries. And as she recounts the process of bringing her serene, perfectly symmetrical porcelain seascape vessels to life, her animated descriptions of its technical steps attest to the process's complexity.

'I use a machine called a jigger-jolly,' she tells me. 'It's an antique piece of machinery that is ordinarily used for mass-producing ceramics, except that I don't want to mass-produce my work; I'm interested in how you can adapt a traditional modelling technique to create something individual. The work then becomes about how you apply clay to the mould, how much water you use, the gestures and the marks that you make, the speed at which the piece is rotating and how the clay is pushed to the side of the mould.'

'It took a long time to develop the technique. I've learned that there are ways of controlling what the landscapes might look like: less water creates a rolling wave; more water creates a creamy slurry that looks like faded clouds – but there's always an element of surprise and occasionally the pieces don't work and I won't like what they look like. Or because it's porcelain, if there's been a draught or they've not been dried slowly enough there will be a little warp in the clay when they're fired.'

'After the first firing, I sand the pieces using a diamond pad to reveal layers of marks. Then once the pieces come out of the kiln for the second time, that's when I polish them, which takes hours. I use six different grades of diamond pad – coarse to fine – to gently buff the ceramic so that the vessels don't have any scratches. It gives the outsides a quality that's a little like marble – they're very smooth and soft. Some might question why I spend the time, but I care about how people enjoy and experience each piece and their tactility is a part of that.'

That interpretation of her work is clearly important to the ceramicist, who is keen that it straddles the artistic and the functional. 'I realised quite early on that I liked making objects that can be used, but I've also chosen to make work that does sit in an interior quietly and neatly. People will inevitably interpret it as they wish.'

The realities and challenges of making a living from art are well documented and I wonder at what point the commercial and the creative collide and how much the notion that a piece needs to sell affects what she creates. 'It's a gamble,' Celia tells me, 'but the pragmatist in me knows that in order to make a career from this it has to work as a business. I have days when I think I'm completely mad. It's difficult investing in myself – it feels scary, but a lot of the biggest hurdles are mainly mental: the worry that I'm not going to be able to carve out an identity through my work.' And then she counters it all by saying that she would produce the work regardless of whether it sold or not. 'I work at a gallery and I teach at a studio and in schools. I think I'll always have to have a job on the side because I don't know when my next body of work will sell, but I just

have to have faith that it will otherwise I'd go mad. I like making things; there's nothing else that I want to do.'

The determination and drive displayed by this talented artist who is bringing the traditions and skills of a heritage craft to a contemporary setting is inspiring, carrying with it a strong sense of optimism that she will find the right balance between creativity and the need to make a living. I feel sure we will indeed be seeing a lot more of her unique, beautiful and calming work.

Celia Dowson's seascape vessels are available to buy in Bamford stores and online: www.bamford.com

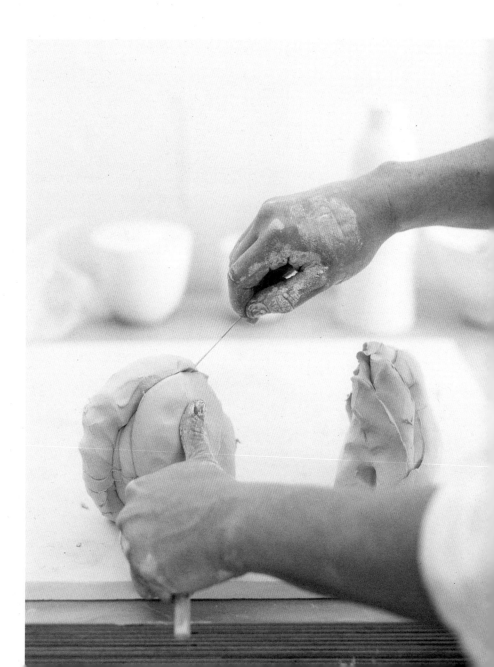

A TABLE
FOR
AUTUMN

PHOTOGRAPHY
Martin Morrell

RIGHT: Daylesford Ludlow
tumblers and jug, grey;
BELOW: Daylesford Palamino
26cm dinner plate, grey;
Palamino 18cm salad plate,
white; Palamino bowl,
13cm, grey

OPPOSITE, clockwise
from bottom left: Daylesford
Westbourne cutlery;
Palamino 26cm dinner plate,
white; Palamino 18cm salad
plate, grey; Palamino bowl,
13cm, white; Ledbury wine
glass, grey; Ludlow tumbler,
grey; plaster leaves
by Viola Lanari

A CELEBRATION OF ENGLISH APPLES

MAKING BIRD FEEDERS

WORDS Leonora Bamford
PHOTOGRAPHY Martin Morrell

I moved to Oxfordshire last year and inherited a beautiful old apple tree which has become the heart of our garden. Britain once produced the most apple varieties in the world, but since the Victorian heyday of knowledgeable and passionate gardeners, so many of the wonderful old varieties have been lost and many orchards have disappeared. The desire for rustic-looking, burnished, knobbly, imperfect-looking fruits has faded, replaced by the more appealing influx of shiny, symmetrical and uniform varieties, and British farmers can't compete with the prices offered by growers in foreign countries. It is a sobering statistic that today approximately 70 per cent of the apples sold in Britain are imported.

Thankfully organisations such as the National Fruit Collection are working to conserve traditional orchards and their wonderful apple varieties and there is a slow and growing interest in protecting and reviving our heritage. Apple Days have become increasingly popular. Annual celebrations of apples and orchards are held throughout October and at these you can often enjoy traditional games such as apple-bobbing, watch demonstrations of cider-making and fruit pressing, and enjoy other entertainment. I can't wait to take the children to one of them this year.

This autumn I am also going to be planting an apple tree or two in our garden; some of my favourite old English varieties are Ashmead's Kernel, Pitmaston Pine, Orleans Reinette and Ribston Pippin and I know they will give our family enormous pleasure. Aside from its beauty, apple blossom is also a rich source of nectar and pollen for our endangered bees and other pollinators, while the trees are a useful habitat and food source for a wide range of wildlife.

Juicing apples, baking them, making crumbles and chutneys are a handful of traditional and wonderful ways to use your apples, but last year the children and I enjoyed drying apple rings, as well as making the adorable bird feeders overleaf. We hung ours close to the kitchen window and it's been so much fun watching the birds at work.

HARVEST

The UK apple season runs from late July to late November, with the main harvesting time being between mid September and late October, depending on the variety. To pick your apples, cup the fruit in the palm of your hand and twist gently. A fully ripe apple should come away from the branch easily.

STORE YOUR APPLES FOR THE WINTER

Store your apples as quickly as possible after they've been picked. Wrap each one in newspaper and place in a crate or cardboard tray in a single layer. Your greengrocer or supermarket will usually be happy to give you some crates or trays, which are useful to allow the apples space to breathe without being piled on top of each other. Special wooden storage racks with drawers are also available to buy. Place the apples in a cool, dry, dark place. Check them regularly and throw away any that start to rot. Most apples should keep well for months if unblemished and properly stored; generally, the later an apple ripens, the better it will keep.

TO MAKE
Bird feeders

YOU WILL NEED:
smooth peanut or almond butter
a mixture of seeds (we used
    pumpkin, sunflower and sesame)
large apples
some long screws
twine

Depending on how many apples you want to hang, mix about 5–6 tablespoons of nut butter with a large handful of seeds. You want the mixture to be thick with seeds.

Cut the apples in half lengthways and hollow out the core with a spoon, knife or a pastry cutter. Fill each hollow with the seed mixture, then pop the apples in the fridge for a couple of hours until firm.

Push a screw into the top of each apple half, tie a piece of twine around the screw and hang from a branch or bird table.

STITCHES IN TIME

WORDS Imogen Fortes
PHOTOGRAPHY Martin Morrell

Knitting is something often associated with a time gone by. It may have been a skill we learned as a child – our mothers, aunts or grandmothers patiently and carefully teaching us how to hold the awkward long needles and gently wind the wool around them, watching proudly as our stitches slowly took shape as a scarf, woolly hat or simply a slightly wonky square. But for many, this slow, seemingly painstaking pastime feels old-fashioned.

There is unquestionably still a very strong tradition of knitting in Scotland and in other coastal communities around the British Isles. True Fair Isle sweaters – with their rows of intricate patterns, knitted on the remote island in Scotland – can have waiting lists of around three years. And although the thick Aran knits traditionally made from soft, undyed yarn, can now be made by machine, the hand-made versions are still highly revered and extremely sought-after. Knitting as a hobby has also enjoyed a renaissance in recent years. As many seek ways to escape the digital world and the constant demands of their phones, the meditative peace and creativity of making something by hand has drawn people to new skills

and knitting groups have sprung up around the country. But where high-end fashion houses and labels once drove the demand to own delicate or elaborately-designed hand-knitted pieces – the skill required to produce these precious items lending them a sense of uniqueness and exclusivity – I wonder how much longer this ancient craft, once interwoven in the fabric of British culture, will be with us.

Stephanie Laird designs and produces exquisite hand-knitted pieces for clothing designers that include Pringle of Scotland, Mulberry, Bamford, Stella McCartney and Paul Smith. She works from her flat, set in a former hospital building in one of the handsome squares in Edinburgh's New Town. Arriving on a calm, bright morning, I am struck by the harmony in the rows of tall, evenly-proportioned sandstone buildings; the elegant uniformity of the Georgian architecture feels like an appropriate setting for someone whose profession is so equally steeped in measured precision and skilled craftsmanship.

'I was a professional ballerina and in my era dancers spent an awful lot of time sitting at the sides during rehearsals. We had a lot of time on our hands and

we generally divided into two groups to fill it – the smokers and the knitters, explains Stephanie. We used to knit our own all-in-ones, just in a very simple stocking stitch, but they had a lovely double V-neck, three-quarter length sleeves and a really low back. They were so beautiful. You put them on over your tights and leotard and they were close-fitting but stretchy and so comfortable.'

'Knitting was just very much part of the dancer's world,' she tells me. 'My mother was a fashion journalist so I have always loved clothes and fabric and I used to work in the wardrobe at the theatre, especially when I was injured. I didn't have any professional training. My mother knits like an angel and so I simply picked it up in childhood; and I have always just understood line and shape. As dancers we all used to take scissors to our leotards – it was nothing to do with vanity, it was about knowing what would give you an extra inch to move; I suppose because we always had to tamper with our bodies, we were very in tune with them. And then when I moved to Edinburgh after my dancing career had ended I met Hillary Rohde, and I started to go to her studio once

a week for the afternoon to help her. Hillary had a company designing two knitwear collections a year, and as a side she would produce hand-knitted pieces for several of the big fashion houses. This was during the 1980s when there was a big trend for hand-knits – it was the heyday when everybody wanted them in their collections, and for a while it was important to have at least one hand-knitted piece, especially for the British designers. Sadly that's not the case now and for most designers knitwear is produced by machine.'

But for a small handful of labels, there is still a value and a beauty to be celebrated in the work of the hand and the intricate skills required to craft hand-knitted pieces. Stephanie works with a collection of knitters, who each work from their own home, mostly in Scotland. 'Hillary had this book – her bible – that I inherited when I took over her company. It is a directory, where she noted the name of each knitter, their address and phone number and what particular skills they had. Some knitters will only do fine knitting, for example; some only chunky; some don't like cashmere because it's slippy, whereas

swool has purchase; some knits are too heavy for my older ladies. We kept a record of all these specifics and learned to work with their different preferences and skills. I know their work so well.'

In a world of digital domination, it's heartwarming to learn how much of the communication between Stephanie and her knitters is still done over the phone and by post. 'Once I have a commission from a designer, I'll work with a pattern maker to draw up the pattern for the design, then I'll ring around my knitters. I'll always send a knitter a sample of the item and say I have a run needing doing and ask how many I can put them down for – two or twenty? It's a conversation. Then I will wind off the yarn, measure it and send them the pattern and sometimes the size – how loosely or tightly a person knits can affect this, so I always spec the pieces for size when they are sent back to me. They will come to me unwashed and often not sewn up, so I'll sew the pieces together.'

'The washing is something that isn't difficult but it takes ages to learn because different yarns need different care. Sometimes I'm terrified the pieces will

stretch or grow during the washing; I lay them so carefully over my pullies. Wool is a little more forgiving than cashmere or alpaca because it gives, so you can change the measurements and shrink or grow the pieces a little according to how you wash and dry them. They take ages to dry – even a cotton knit takes about a week and a half. Then I stitch on the labels and send them to the designer.'

As many people shun the ubiquity and uniformity that comes from buying something that's been produced by machine in vast numbers, craftsmanship and artistry are enjoying a welcome revival in popularity. But unlike a ceramic or a piece of glassware, where a flaw might be part of an object's charm, I ask whether Stephanie ever notices mistakes in the knitters' work and whether that means the piece has to be reworked. 'Sometimes I'll be at the stage where I'm packaging up the piece and then I'll realise there's a mistake. Once it's been washed you can't re-knit with the yarn so that piece has to be knitted again, but sometimes I'm able to fix a small mistake myself; it depends on the pattern – the simpler a pattern, the more mistakes show up as there are

fewer places to hide. But I believe hand-knits shouldn't have to be carbon copies – as long as the mistake won't make it likely to wear or unravel, to me those tiny imperfections are part of what makes it special.'

'Circular knitting – where there are no seams – is particularly difficult, however,' Stephanie tells me, 'because it all has to join up. You start at the bottom of a sweater and finish with the arm holes and if you lose your concentration and miss one row then you have to unravel it and start all over again.'

It's hard to imagine how it's not very lonely or very isolating as a profession. 'I think it is isolating,' Stephanie says. 'Sometimes when I call one of my ladies I'll be on the phone for an hour and a half. Some will call you all the time to ask what you think, question a technicality or simply to tell you how a piece is looking. Others you don't hear a squeak from and the sweaters come back three weeks later looking impeccable.' She also tells me that some of these women just need to knit; they find it incredibly comforting. 'I have a lady in her nineties who knits baby things for me and I think she just knits all day long. They're all very different women; but they're all so brilliant at it.'

As our conversation continues, I sense a note of sadness as she talks about the future of the craft and the profession. 'I don't think anyone I work with is under 60. One lady was trained in the old-fashioned way at her country primary school in Ireland, and that just isn't part of anybody's culture anymore. All my knitters were taught by their mothers or aunts or grandmothers but the skill is no longer being passed on in that way,' Stephanie says. 'And even though there have been surges in demand for hand-knits through passing trends for fishermen sweaters or big chunky knits;

the finer things take so long to knit and are complicated so the fashion labels don't want to wait. We're all in too much of a hurry.'

'I have beautiful fine knits that nobody would know how to make now. Baby blankets are knitted as 1-ply (a single strand of wool) and the knitters who have the delicate hands or the knowledge to do that are like fairies; the needles are so tiny – virtually nobody has that skill anymore. There is also a lot that can now be done by machine,' she concedes, 'even intarsia (in which a separate length or ball of yarn is used for each area of colour in the pattern), but a lot can only be done by hand. And though you can do something very pretty by machine, and perhaps something extraordinary, there are still stitches that only a human hand can fashion.'

I am moved by the passion and love with which Stephanie describes not only each piece she makes, but the craft itself. 'Knitting is extraordinary,' she says. 'You can knit with anything: I remember making knitted ribbon skirts for Pringle; and there's a wonderful tradition of using what you've got – knitting with scraps of material to make rugs. I'm very grateful to have been part of this world and it's just so sad to think that once that skill is lost, it's lost, and we'll never retrieve it. Eventually somebody will take an interest, do lots of research and revive the stitches and the stories behind them but probably not in my lifetime.'

And indeed I wonder whether those skills can ever be reproduced to replicate the detail in the pieces she shows me; and the knowledge that was once passed from one generation to the next preserved. I fear it might be several generations before children today grow up wearing the thick, slightly scratchy, hand-knitted jumpers, as my sister and I were lucky enough to do.

ENCOUNTERING EVOLUTION

EXPLORING THE GALÁPAGOS ISLANDS

WORDS Carole Bamford
PHOTOGRAPHY Anthony, Carole and George Bamford

We wake at first light. The dawn will just be breaking as we climb up on deck to be met by a pale pink sky, the silver disc of the full moon still high above the horizon. All we can hear is the rip of the waves, the plop of the odd fish, the frigate birds flying overhead. It's just the calm silence of nature; meditative and tranquil. Then as the sun slowly rises to take the moon's place, our day exploring would begin.

The Galápagos islands are known for their remoteness. Their closest point to any mainland is around 1,000 kilometres from Ecuador's coastline, and travelling there you do feel like you have reached the end of the earth. There's no interference: no background hum of traffic or electricity or any form of interruption; very little technology; just the peace and calming beauty of the natural world.

The archipelago – a group of 19 islands, of which four are inhabited – is known for its unique animal species. I learn that of the 2,900 species of marine animals in the islands' surrounding waters, a quarter are endemic, the majority now endangered. Galápagos sea lions, marine and land iguanas, flightless cormorants, whale sharks, the most northerly species of penguin and the giant lumbering tortoises which give the islands their name, are just some of the extraordinary native wildlife that leave me humbled by the beauty, diversity and complexity of the natural world.

Our days are divided between exploring the land and the water. In the morning we put on our masks and snorkels and set off swimming behind a guide. Within moments we are surrounded by shoals of fish; so close we can reach out to touch them. Then one of us will motion and point at something excitedly – a vast black and white ray or a shark, not just one but two or three. And yet we feel remarkably at ease – even my youngest grandchildren, with whom we're travelling, not frightened, just in awe, grateful to be in such close proximity to these graceful wild creatures.

You lose yourself in the
landscapes and in the enormity
of what you're seeing

Then in the afternoon we go for a hike. As we step off the boat, a melody of birdsong and mating calls fills the air. And as we begin the trek up the trail into the volcanic heights, our eye will be caught by a streak of turquoise – the islands' famous blue-footed boobies, or the languorous stretch of an iguana we'd mistaken for lava, basking in the sun. It is a bird watcher's paradise and I lose count of the number of different species I see.

I am struck by the variety of the ancient landscape. Some islands look very barren – dark, bare mounds rising out of the clear bright waters, while others are carpeted in lush green forest, and yet they're less than 10 kilometres apart. And in turn I wrestle with comprehending how the animals and birds adjust themselves to their habit – each island has its own unique set of species. It is these extraordinary paradoxes that fascinated Darwin and so many others after him. Like them I am in awe of this extraordinary encounter with evolution – this opportunity to be witness to its changes and its power at such close quarters.

There aren't really words to describe one's feelings or experience of visiting the Galápagos – amazing, or beautiful are words we keep repeating but they cannot begin to scratch the surface. You lose yourself in the landscapes and in the enormity of what you're seeing. Above all I'm left with an overwhelming sense of humility and gratitude: to be granted this gift of watching nature at work. The laws of survival are vivid: you watch the chase of a prey and marvel at nature's harmony; and it teaches you things.

And yet, I am conscious that we have an enormous responsibility in travelling here. Although it is believed that around 95 per cent of the islands' pre-human biodiversity remains intact, the Galápagos ecosystem is fragile and vulnerable to the impact of human contact, and the increased tourism to the island does inevitably pose threats. Support for the continued conservation efforts and sustainable development are vital if the area is to be protected and preserved. A visit to this otherworldly archipelago truly is a life-changing experience, but we must remain passive, fleeting witnesses to all it can teach us.

SOULS
FROM THE SEA

WORDS Carole Bamford
PHOTOGRAPHY Martin Morrell

I've collected pebbles and shells since I was a little girl. My childhood is dappled with the sunlit memories of holidays at the beach and I recall those hours spent combing the shoreline as cherished moments of independence. Granted the freedom to roam the section of the beach closest to my parents, my fingers and eyes would scour the floor in search of treasures to fill my small basket. But as I've grown older the symbolism of the act of searching itself has grown and gathered as much importance and significance to me as the pebbles themselves.

Collecting stones has become a meditation, a way of quietening and freeing my busy mind, leaving me with the most profound sense of contentment and relaxation. It is a feeling I have never been able to recapture in anything else I do. To the amusement and partial bewilderment of my family, I will still devote hours of our holidays to wandering the beach, my eyes fixed on the ground around me, scanning the colours and forms and textures. And I am not alone in my seaside forays; many others share my passion.

Lots of people tread on stones and shells without even noticing them but for me they are so much more than the floor on which I walk. I believe stones have souls. Stones have travelled – they've been tumbled and rocked by tumultuous tides; they are a sign of nature's resilience. Perhaps it's this timelessness, this sense of permanency and strength that draws me to them. Holding a stone in my hand gives me a strong feeling of connection to nature – it is grounding and calming, a physical reminder of the solidity and eternal quality of the earth beneath our feet.

There is, of course, the ethical dilemma of removing items from the beach. In many places it is prohibited and I will gently but reluctantly return my gathered treasures to the waves, but those that have been lifted are stored in labelled boxes, as precious and valuable to me as the family photographs that adorn so many tables and corners of our house. And I find reassurance knowing that one day they will be returned to the earth.

I once stumbled upon a pebble shaped like a heart that fit perfectly into the palm of my hand. I have always loved the shape of hearts; their symbolism makes me feel happy, and finding a heart-shaped stone or shell is still a particularly special moment. They are a small but ever-expanding part of my collection.

Seed

From star to star, from sun and spring and leaf,
And almost audible flowers whose sound is silence,
And in the common meadows, springs the seed of life.

Now the lilies open, and the rose
Released by summer from the harmless graves
That, centuries deep, are in the air we breathe,
And in our earth, and in our daily bread.

External and innate dimensions hold
The living forms, but not the force of life;
For that interior and holy tree
That in the heart of hearts outlives the world
Spreads earthly shade into eternity.

– Kathleen Raine